Vellum Leaves
& Lettered Skins

Colleen Anderson

Vellum Leaves and Lettered Skins © 2025 by Colleen Anderson

Published by Raw Dog Screaming Press
Bowie, MD

First Edition

Cover art copyright 2025 by
Book Layout by Jennifer Barnes

Printed in the United States of America

ISBN: 978-1-947879-93-5
Library of Congress Control Number:
2025942116

RawDogScreaming.com

Dedication

Depression is a very real and debilitating condition. Those who are stuck in the towers of isolation cannot always reach out. We must do so through compassion and education. To every person who has been captive in a tower, whatever form that tower took.

Contents

Dedication 3
An Introduction 7
A Vegetal Greed 13
Weeds 15
Tower 16
Locks 18
Tree 21
Gorgon 23
Godiva 26
Sedna 28
Shear 30
Leaves 31
Forgotten Language 33
Small Reveals 35
Let Me 36
Transformation 39
Vegetable Love 40
Honey 42
Egg 44
First Bud 45
Tempest 47
Descent 50
Shedding 52
Sand 54
Weave 56

Ripening	58
Labor	60
Fruiting Bodies	63
Seeking	66
Seasons	68
Sargasso	71
Garden	73
Wreath	75
Bleeding Hearts	78
In the End	80
Adrift	81
Full Circle	82
Loom	84
Reflection	86
Seeds	88
Spring	90
Tide	92
Tapestry	95
Autumn	97
Winter	100

Vellum Leaves & Lettered Skins
An Introduction

by Jonathan Maberry

I write for a living.

I read to be alive.

Ever since I was a kid reading has been the thing that has allowed me to live more lives than the one I have. It allows me to be more people than is possible in a single incarnation. It allows me to have more viewpoints, more insights, more experiences, then one life can provide.

I know I'm not alone in this. There are, thankfully, plenty of people who consider themselves Readers with a capital R. Not just book people, but readers of all kinds of work, readers who delight in the variety of ways in which thought can be expressed and art can be explored. That variety has often been at the core of my own career decisions. Going from wanting to be an intrepid newspaper reporter who broke the big story and tore down the corrupt whatever to a magazine feature writer, to a playwright, to a writer of sarcastic greeting cards, to the author of mass market books on subjects ranging from martial arts to folklore, to a novelist, to a short story writer, and to a poet.

All of those ways of expressing myself have been reflections of seeing how other writers reflect their own experiences and insights through whatever method of storytelling feels best to them in the moment. Some people like the straight, unfiltered clarity of nonfiction, whether that be an article on how to do something or an essay on why something has been done. Some people like the brevity of short works where they can go in and play for a bit, experiment, try new things, and then step out leaving the reader a juicy slice but not the whole pie. Some people like the elegance and ornamentation of a lush novel, where many different thoughts can be expressed through the actions and words of a large cast of characters propelled into different situations. And some people find that the best way to tell the story that burns in their mind is to cast it into verse.

This book is that latter kind.

Colleen Anderson has taken a story that we all know. Or... think we know. And that right there, that approach, is one of the most magical things about writing. That we can take any story, whether drawn from mythology, religion, folk tales, urban legends, whatever... and reframe it, editing elements of that story without changing its essential nature. They take something you think you know and by polishing it and playing with it and running it through the filters of their unique mind, create a new version of it for a new generation. Hollywood often tries to do this and falls into the trap of pandering. Some novelists make the mistake of trying to chase a trend or recapture lightning in a bottle, only to fall into the different trap of cliche and imitation.

This book is not either of those things.

What Colleen has done here is to take a story so fundamental that most of us could recite it, if not in the exact words but in phrasing enough to be able to convey what that story was. And God knows we've seen enough adaptations of it, and enough pop culture references to it, that we think we know the story. But a good storyteller knows how to take the expected and present it but to encourage the reader to look closer, think more deeply, and discover new riches.

All the way to the end of this book I found references, some overt some oblique, to other things. Little bits of folklore, themes from classic poetry of another century, and so on. Not to rest upon those classic works, but to reinvigorate them in a way that is both subtle and effective. There is for example, a reference in here to the *Lady of Shalott* –though that name is never explicitly given. Like many well-read poets, Colleen knows her classics, and she honors Alfred Lord Tennyson's 19th century poem of doomed love in the age of Camelot, but twists it gently to make it fit seamlessly into the narrative of Rapunzel. That is not an easy thing to do, and it is very difficult to do it well.

She does in very well indeed.

In my epic fantasy novels, the Kagen the Damned series, I've also borrowed openly and with some degree of reverence that same poem, and others. I even had a Loreena McKennitt playlist running while I wrote those scenes. I had the same playlist on while reading *Vellum Leaves and Lettered Skins*.

It's fun to reach back and touch those classic works. People do it all the time. After all *West Side Story* and *Buffy the Vampire Slayer* are both based on *Romeo and Juliet* by Shakespeare. And yet they are unique, complete in their uniqueness, and are not in any way copies. That takes a level of confidence to be able to have inside an overall work of reference to some other work, and yet do it in a way that is completely celebratory. It's also fun for well versed readers to be able to find those little Easter eggs, those juicy nuggets of literary reference.

What makes this even more fun is how those elements are seeds from which an extraordinary new thing grows. The poems in this book are like chapters of the novel. They can each stand alone as a fine bit of poetry. Collectively they conspire to draw us into a new version of an adventure we thought we knew completely. The reader in me absolutely loved it. I've read it on my balcony looking out at trees. And I read it again on the beach watching dolphins swim in crystal blue waters. I will likely read it again, perhaps in a year, because with certain poets you know for sure that even one or two readings, however thoroughly one pays attention, does not yield all the fruit to be found.

When I was young, Ray Bradbury introduced me to poetry. He gave me a copy of *The New Oxford Book of English Verse 1250–1950* for my 14th birthday.

"What's so big about this stuff?" I asked, and was quite serious about it. To me, the only poetry that mattered were song lyrics. The schools I'd attended to that point were lower-income blue collar institutions that never spent much time on poetry. I mean, yes, they were part of our curriculum, but only a small part. Little was said about nuance, about metaphor and underlying meaning, no time was spent teaching us how to decode the subtleties of figurative and descriptive language. So, I felt my question was valid.

Instead of mocking my question, Bradbury sat me down in a corner and began telling me *about* poetry. He explained how poets possess an enviable talent for brevity and concision. He, of course, had to explain brevity and its value, but he made his point.

He said, "A poet can take the most complex emotion and distill it down to a few lines that often tells us more than a whole chapter of prose. And it does so in a way that invites the reader to help conjure the images and grasp the concepts."

He went on—then and at other times—to school me on the basics of imagery and allegory, metaphor and hyperbole, and lots of other aspects of language, assuring me that if I wanted to be a good writer of short stories and novels, then I should become a student of poetry.

Nowadays, I read poetry aloud every day before I work on my prose. And every day it enriches my understanding of the world, nature, people, magic, possibilities, and beauty.

When I read Colleen Anderson's book, I read it aloud.

Every poem.

And in that process, I could *feel* each poem come alive. Individually, and as a whole. As a story told in verse.

They are beautiful poems. Smooth without ever being slick; accessible without being shallow; compelling without being preachy. They tell many stories and in doing so tell one complete story.

I actually envy you if you're reading this for the first time. More so if you're reading Colleen's poetry for the first time. There is a certain joy in discovering the new. A new writer, a new voice, a new set of artistic insights, new sensibilities, and new magic.

There is magic here.

I recommend you give yourself a nice little block of time, something soothing to drink, something beautiful to look at, and then open this book and begin to read. It's worth setting the stage for the experience.

Enjoy.

Jonathan Maberry
San Diego, June 2025

A Vegetal Greed

My earliest memories are not of a tower
but seeded with visions, half images
plants pulsing, luscious plump fruit
yet, my story always begins with theft

A woman, some women, a girl
a child—was it me trying to fill
my hollow with insatiable need
a vegetal greed

A jungle—mauve-flowered rapunzel
sharp rampion, bitter parsley
even the juicy red Asian jujube
and its sister the plum
tantalizing, nature's allure

The invasive species, was it them or we
traded me to the witch, the aunt
the nuns, the trolls? payment
in vengeance she acquires me, plants
with sweet words, waters with caution

Perhaps it was my mother's need
when I still swam in her womb
or Aunty's verdant garden

that carpets the land with secrets
still I hunger

I watch from the tower window
crave that emerald paradise
those promises of probing darkness
untangling roots hidden within
Earth's fertility, its tenacious green

I long to consume mountainous salads
be soothed not by stone
but with bare feet to walk, stroll, caper
across that renewing swath
writhe sated in swaying grasses

I want to fall to the earth
a wild new seed, sun nurtured
following no prescribed path
spread rapaciously alive
and devour a bounty of tales

Weeds

Aunty says I'm growing like a weed
her glance is already scything her garden
for intruders that should be uprooted

She inspects the ordered rows
like troops I view far afield
stalwart turnips, sturdy carrots
blustery parsley

She looks askance at me
gangly, a pale sprout in the tower
crowned with cornsilk hair
not worth the wind that touches it

I've seen Aunty review her greens
like the generals with their troops
the stragglers, the weak culled
wildflowers, heads snapped off
tossed in the ditch

What am I when I stop growing
will she cultivate a golden treasure
consume my songs and aspirations
      or see me an unsightly weed?

Tower

The turret looms
    always

Over
    my thoughts
this thing alive
  its walls my ribcage
  my stalwart spine
    always
holding me up
  impenetrable

Ever since monks clambered
  in   pulled up their ladders
to save their skins
from blonde-haired invaders
  plowers of earth, raiders seeking
    tender flesh and softer gold
    bright gems to pry free
bodies to plunder but for this spire

Only it could withstand their axes
this age-old conglomerate stone

My tower
could be that bastion
a citadel
    to keep beloveds safe
and chattels in

Perhaps it is an older sibling
    I never knew
but of late
this edifice
   is more a mummified soldier
   a ravenous troll
       clutching me with malaise
these stone ribs
a gate   a barrier
no confidante to give advice

The windows, my eyes into the world
   the heart is nothing
     I am a contracting muscle

My feet are nothing
but stone, sediment
   I cannot run
from the unending vista
   the restrictive corseting

This tower
each stone each boulder
   mortars me in
this cage

Locks

Aunty never cut my hair
perhaps to enjoy the luxury
where her own bristly, defiant bush
was more akin to untamed weeds

Each day these golden fronds
     reached toward the light
     freedom of the open fields
I loved their waves
the cascades like a pale sea

When my hair reached my feet
it began to gather life
     ladybirds and beetles
         even the small sparrow's nest

I played games in solitude
braiding, winding, even weaving
this plaited kudzu vine
when my locks doubled in length

At first, I created childhood whimsies
hid corn dollies
wheaten waifs within my tresses

Then I wove fences, baskets,
cages for the living
and other forms of binding
as I sought to define my space

I trapped them all
robins, goldfinches, fat bees
mice and one green snake
saddened when they held no secrets
I shook free their fragile bones

Years crawled onto Aunty's back
as she bent to time's weight
she dispensed with aerial magics
commanded me to form a ladder

Did she leave my hair flowing
so she could ascend my golden stair
or believe it burdened me to stay

Keep me entangled in images
of a fairytale life, a hoarded treasure
or as dues for her long-pilfered greens

Without my hair, like Samson
would I be nothing of worth
would I matter at all

Would I be another
abandoned child tossed to the wind
to settle on my own

It is a fantasy I keep

—One day soon
I shall weave the key
      that will spring the lock
      that is my hair

Tree

A tree's life spans centuries
many branches
forking to tell a variety of tales
the journey—many lifetimes
toward the sun to survive
the weevil, and hailstorm beatings

It canopies the forest families
fluttering blossoms upon peridot leaves
shade dappling me
in the cool sigh of arboreal slumber

These leaves—these parchment scrolls
books—a thousand stories
carry me along on imaginary wings
feathered, membraned, scaled
to lands of the past, old gods, fey beings

Secrets inked in script
crow breath, blossom death, fire teeth
caterpillar scrape and gnaw
nests dropping eggshell shards

I only imagine the song of trees
see them from afar,

the network nourishes
as years grow with visions
my shelves burdened

This fabricated forest
a veneer
enclosing me
in other worlds
adventures I yearn to pick

There are cankers, galls forming
where bark sloughs and slips
the tree sawed and hacked
until the expanse emerges
beyond the canopied protection

I see the tales falling
leaves curling, dying
the skeleton of limbs now reaching
ever reaching toward a distant sun
to escape the blight
of fantasies felled by reality

Gorgon

A woman was fated
to be wed to the animal kingdom
her crown, serpents
bent on deceiving or perhaps protecting

She lived in ruins
shunned from former society
leery of her formidable power
She could mind her own
her family of snakes
be partially content

Men, heroes they're called
saw only a quest
a task to challenge her independence
to live without their will
their knowledge their love
their lusts

Removed from their realm
their influence, they couldn't bear it,
chose to label her monster
unable to believe any woman
wouldn't see them as lord or god

They infiltrated her lair
She won the battles so often, turning away
disgusted at yet another statue
displaying brutality, masculinity
warriors always bent on being
number one

Yet she was lonely
not able to find a good soul
So she tried conversation
sometimes a sphinxian riddle
sought a light behind their eyes
They didn't like that

Then she honed her serpent tongue
to armour against brash invaders
When they approached, the snakes
lashed with acute observation
spitting out an accurate fact—
inferior chin, nasally voice
childish giggle, or odd lapses
during engaging talks

When they went for the jugular
called out her sybaritic ways
she returned in kind
striking fast—
their responses leaden as stone

Thus, she became neither happy
nor discontent but continued her days
fishing, creating garments of the earth
talking with her sisters and snakes

These conquerors only saw
what had to be tamed
She knew it would spell her end
and planned, weaving tales
that kept her and her family safe
behind a fearsome myth
that she was already dead

Godiva

She rode naked on a horse
through village
streets and countryside
protesting taxes
robed in flowing, silken hair
unpinned, a garment unadorned

She knew her lands
the people who toiled
the balance of power
used her nature-born tools
to bring about change

>My hair rustles winding, writhing
>moving restless to find a way
>a vine that hears the paths of mice and mite
>bird and vole, these small lives
>nurturing joy and fear in splendid purity

>I will twine and twist, trailing down the walls
>send whispers to the beetles scuttling
>through the mortar, follow footprints
>left in flour, taste the dust upon the panes
>learn the ways of those beyond these walls

My hair will flow through street, village
into valleys, curl in swallows' nests
and tickle ears of sleeping cats
let the breeze play freely with the tendrils
in this way I, too, will know my lands

Sedna

Always tried to be her own self
rebellious
daughter willing to swim
the depths
to see to see to the sea

Her father chose for her a bird
a raptor as her suitor, to be prey
her avian husband
she refused, would never settle
nor be pleased
with the leavings
morsels for men

So the loving father took her
on a day trip hunting
in the kayak far from shore
he pushed her over the edge
her only lifeboat
clinging to what she knew
the life she was about to leave

He pulled an axe and cleaved
her fingers, knuckles, let her fall
divvying up her body, sacrifice

to men and birds
a cowardly father

She settled deep upon the ocean floor
fingers, knuckles drifting down
her fury transmuted into freedom
severed limbs to surging sea life

Her hair fanned out
a seal, fish, and whale haven
fantail, kelp-haired woman
once despised
who never could be controlled

Protector of the ocean realms
vengeful goddess
who does not trust the ways of men

They must appease, pay in treasures
or delve deep to comb her vast hair

Only then, if she chooses
will she permit some of the sea
to fill those mortal mouths
and in turn she will feed
on them as well

Shear

A mighty warrior
wore tresses like a girl
envied for his iron might
from hair that never met a blade
because this growth held his oath

Then a woman sheared him
betrayal on his scalp
shame surfacing as fame dissipated
along with heroic deeds

My hair is ten times that length
yet, it is I who am locked away
with weighty golden skeins
is it my power or my handicap

Who then will betray me
remove my locks
will I be set free
once I am shorn

 A sheep separated from the herd
able to roam freely?

Leaves

My bookcases hold
a hundred spines, faces turned from me
   until I coax them, tales it seems
   they do not wish to tell

Yet they do—these foreign realms
like green fields speckled with tiny cattle
glimpsed from my trellised window
   places of fire and swords
   of grief and abandonment

These vellum leaves and lettered skins
whisper of other lives
   times strange, magical
    adventurous, whimsical

I lose myself for days
wandering the inked landscapes
seeking to understand
   absentmindedly, I unravel hair for her ascent
   barely aware when she brings me food

Scrolls with secrets unrolling
across my divan
I strain to trace the messages between the lines

the mysteries I'm sure are hidden there
   scribed with invisible ink

Of late she comments on me staring
blank faced, looking at emptied shelves
   as the moments and dramas play
     upon my eyes' canvas

Books and parchments cascade
   I kneel, clawing at their leather backs
     to reveal more

I weep and flip sheets
turn tomes upside down
   plead again for the revelation
     secreted from me

The answers fall out of reach
   fluttering away, like leaves
     Autumn is always the season of leaving

Then the concept appears
     not within the flattened pages
   where I've endlessly been searching

For the first time I breathe in
that most precious word
    escape
and winter freezes everything
   in tableaux

Forgotten Language

crumble dust, powder despair
I gouge mortar holding stone bones
press my ear to gritty walls
whitewash flaking
what's hidden appears in cracks
tiny voices scratch at the floors
old wood splinter-fine

mouse beetle butterfly bee
learn to speak in ancient tongues
scribe the language with stone and nail

even Aunty with her incantations
doesn't know this secret jargon

tell me, I whisper, click and trill
of the world beyond these walls
is it dangerous, is it sweet
are there monsters lurking to feast
can I wander woods, trails, boggy fields
are there tricks in learning to thrive

they twitch or flex chitinous wings
rub furred paws, quiver the air
with buzz, hum, and chirrup

Colleen Anderson

their revelations
more aware than me

it is all you've hoped and more besides
it is wonder, light and terror

there are nightmares for our size
large birds that dive
snakes that swallow
foxes slippery and sly
all feed upon our families

we breed in wild green, flowers
seeds, live free, move mostly unseen
winds serenade, leaf litter
trees, hives hold our homes

not many hear our words
nor any yours—you are the bee
without the hive, mouse without
a tribe, or place to meet your kind

we speak with you
a shade to the outside world
you might never be free
but we will listen
to your pleas

Small Reveals

Eye-shaped apple seed
Wind-whispered birch leaf

Sun-polished beetle back
Shadow-tinted dove feather

Sun-stained mouse bone

Ghost-stitched spider thread
Angel-dropped dust mote

I plead to each

Their secrets of entry to guide me
Out of this locked room

Let Me

see the fields
        You can view them from the window

touch milk thistle leaves, be stung by bees
fondle silky petals, inhale ripe cypress
blow frosty breath into the sky

        I will bring you bouquets, a feast for your eyes

walk outside, cool grass licking my feet
feel the undulations of the earth
the sun-warmed pastures
pebbles biting if I transgress

        It's too wild, there are unknowns

embrace the unknown, inhale the unexpected
breathe in mystery, shiver in fear or wonder
see the animals move through the forest

        It's ferocious and will maim

But you do it!

I have experience

experience the world, move in my own ways
gain knowledge of the season's cycles
feel the hard cold rain

You're too young

When will I be old enough

Never! I cherish you too much

If so, then let me be free
So that rough bark may bruise my skin
that dew will stain my hem
that sun's hot touch will enflame me
that wind will comb my hair
that ants will dance over my feet
that the pear I pluck will gift me nectar

I will bring you a cornucopia of fruit, colors,
flavors: you will never want

I want to be on my own

You would not survive

cut my hair, unburden me

No

Why is my hair so important?

> *It ties me to you; our bond is strong*

Is it magic, this ropy length?

> *It is your beauty*

Is my beauty not me?

> *I will bring you jewels*

Is my beauty not me?

> *I must tend my garden*

Transformation

I am tired of this prison
its silent, stifling walls
      one cruel window
to remind I am removed
an eagle's envy aerie
      only stories fly free, not me

I will no longer be soft flesh
contained
shall molt into a scorpion
climb the pitted surface of these stones
so unlike my life's featureless land
navigate the terrain as if it were my skin

I will bathe in cool lunar light
as my pincers glisten, sharpen
I will thrust them into unknown crevices

I will shear the shades of gray
this thick air
the mortar that sinks me in miasma

then I shall venture
stinger raised
afraid of nothing

Vegetable Love

Nights with naught but stars watching
winking
do they know my thoughts
my longing, an ache day in day out
so much time desiccating my thoughts
planted with tales
ideas set to germinate with tender administration

I explore, walk fingertips over the only landscape
I've been allowed to know
the smooth hills, warm plains, valley of my thighs
with sighs I open under the sky
the window my witness
cooling me as I seek completion

inclusion within a whole to be a part
each day the cornucopia arrives
fertile vegetables, sweet deep green cucumber
carrots daring darkness, aubergines sleek and foreign
zucchini meeting middle ground
what I don't consume I use

We have a kinship
aside from beetles, mice and birds
they are confidantes

I whisper to them of my hopes and fantasies

Sometimes I wish them silent
unseeing, willing to please
my vegetable kingdom to serve at my command

I sigh, wander my fingers over flesh
slide their sleek skins against mine
they always seek my moisture
slake my burning thirst

my hope that love be more
than vegetable companions
as I open wider, waiting
to accept new seeds

Honey

Consider me a flower, a tree
a sacred fruit
some days, I am petals floating
others, in bloom burgeoning
smothering perfume

The day is honey-heavy with bees
sleep strokes my eyes in hazy heat
I doze and drone, abuzz with humming desires
until I hear: *Rapunzel, Rapunzel*

And now the dream, an insect caught
in resined amber, I crawl from my somnolent state
a flower trembles in the orchard
a black-eyed bird watches, leaves

I'm reluctant to scatter these sweet visions
I take my weighted, golden anchor
twist it twice around the hook
toss it cascading over mortared walls

I barely notice, yawning, fading away
a soft breath, a draft until stillness enfolds
bees, birds, even the scratchy leaves of trees

    Silence…
    this is the moment
    everything changes

Bees alight, feet dancing over petals
he is robed gold, burgundy, and brown
a flutter, I gasp, he is the breeze
bursting sweet songs bred
his mouth murmuring thrumming
my skin vibrating
I stare speechless—suspended
waiting to see
will I be stung
pollinated

    But he is no bee
    and I no flower

Will he take and leave me
shall we drink each the other's nectar
explore his bright shadows painting his clothes
we circle each other
wary, will he taste and leave
will my need drive me blindly

His touch warms
I turn to languid, flowing
heat-filled honey

Egg

I am encased
my centre holds summer's sun
waiting to pour forth

I look out the trellised window
roses, daisies lazily waving
to the sky's azure canopy
birds looping lightly
settling in their nests

I am ready now
to crack this casing
push my way through
sing of light and love
take new steps

Fly into adventure
bring others my radiance

First Bud

With him near, each day flowers strange
ethereal, blooms fill my eyes, my throat
I choke on perfume till it pours from me
vibrant blue vibrating
on the verge of something else

The window frames my world
brings arabesques of sparrow, robin, swallow
I shiver in summer warmth
cool at his remembered touch
that flared my skin

He ascends each day while Aunty is away
I don't mind his weight
as we soar lofty heights, explore
new landscapes, unaware of anything
but how we redefine our borders

In short bursts I tell him of my tiny world
stories that sheathe me
my shelf of tales, pressed on leaves
the simple songs of birds and crickets

He opens windows to many lands
I have never seen a ribbon

span the length of a life so lived
through places that wind the world

The tower's thick stone disintegrates
as we mold new horizons
fashion different histories
our laughter rising, nightingale song

When Aunty brings me my bedtime snack
and loosens my lacing
I sigh and smile, it was so tight

Aunty stops, the temperature drops
I shiver, pull my robe closed
something's wrong

She flies out the window
scrolls sucked into her wake
she hasn't done so since I was twelve

It's midsummer eve
I lay wrapped in a shawl
quivering as something else stirs

Tempest

Winter comes early
Her cold words whip through the window
rough wind thrusts me forward
the window's precipice nears

> *You wanted the world*
> *It is yours*

                Wait! What did I do?

I claw mortared stone for purchase
tangling in my undone hair

> *You broke my rules*
> *My heart*

                I never knew your rules!

> *You were mine*

                What does that mean?
                Was I not family?

> *To cherish, for me alone to love*

          Do you love me?
          Even if I also love another?

Only I was to love you; you were mine

Her words lacerate my hands, my face
I cower in the anchor of my hair

          You keep saying that
          I was only your possession
          Like one of your flowers

More than that, less than that

          Less? You're my family!

She spins around, a spiral of spite

You were all that I had

          Had? I'm still here
          So are the flowers

You are nothing to me

I'm pummelled and pulled
through the window, tumbling in clouds

I scream, shriek at the rending
hair whipping like angry snakes

        You will rue this day
        I still have my prince

Her voice a ghost in the air

    You are naïve—I cast you
    To wander your days alone in the desert

        I'd rather be there than with my jailer!

Her face, a shock of wide eyes, soured mouth

    Then be gone

Dampened by cloud dew
my eyes pool with loss, regret

Chilled by night's laugh
I twirl and whirl into dust
storms of grit and sand scratch me
eyes tearing, throat parching

I am alone, abandoned

        Am I free?

Descent

    A girl who was a goddess
    loved the flowers
    their scents perfuming her world
    she only knew of growth
    everblooming joy
    her watchful loving mother

    Until she plucked that narcissus
    fragrant, lovely, irresistible

My watchful witch was not loving
daisies and roses remained captive
in a vase, their scent's fading
my heart hardening into a seed

The prince and I, we too tasted
the orchid and the bee

    The land cracked apart
    and she fell into the arms
    of a god who ruled the unchanging
    land of the dead

    She could only return from time to time
    having tasted of his seed

We have taken the plunge
I've fallen from the tower
banished to the wastelands
my prince missing or dead

Aunty never was a goddess
I will never return

Shedding

I sloughed the tower
cloistered life, entrapping tresses
I had outgrown like snakeskin
their own special lock

Ready to blindly seek the unknown
Aunty creaking shrieking
the wind at my back
she cast me from the nest

I had wanted to test wings
yet flightless from the bower
upon which my love had alighted
I plummeted into a different world

The warm hand of the prince
years sealed within stones
left their imprint
a mark I couldn't shed

Furrowed I've been sent to float
sink, land in lands unknown
yearning for that one safe room again
the familiar borders

A wild beating in my chest
though I am exiled, loosed
to wander, to wonder unfamiliar
this freedom thrust upon me

I had been content, a loving creature
but now I am more alone
the witch having locked my past
the prince deserted, I know not where

Now I exist digging deep within
the shifting sands for cactus roots
and hidden gems of water
seeking shelter from night's cold kiss

I fall upon rats and lizards
unheedingly rend, tearing
with fingers cracked and scaled
slither from sun's rough touch

My past hisses away in sand
these demons whisper
what have you sown
what will you reap

I have only this skin
to shed, to grow accustomed to
and soon, soon I will have
other mouths to feed

Colleen Anderson

Sand

Sand chokes me
infiltrating with gritty surety
    every crease, fold, opening
it plants its slippery seeds
each grain, invasive

my thoughts trickle away
hopes of a life
    pillowed with comfort and people
    and love—

this howling reverse sea
I drown in dryness
never thought seclusion could penetrate
    me deeper
than when I suffocated
    in the tower

But it does

the tower is isolated
but now I'm scoured
    under the pale sky
        and its partner's great white eye
snakes hiss in disdain

scorpions rattle carapaces
taunting

You don't belong here

I want to leave
as I did the tower
    my way was lost
        before I ever found it

If only these arid creatures
supplicant cacti
bleached bones
would point the way
      away
from these desiccating dunes

If only I could escape these daily abrasions
grow wings
      fly free of towers, burdens, hair
           shifting sand

Weave

With teeth and sharpened gems
unearthed raw
I tear at my hair
its length a sweltering chain
I cannot bear

My belly a boulder
weighing me with a future
heavier than my past
I do not abandon this gift and curse
but gather the honeyed strands

At night I weave them
into blankets, baskets, a wide-brimmed hat
when not diving for lizards, pulverizing scorpions
roasting cacti on rocks

I live in extremes
from that cloistered tower
to this uncontained expanse
day melts me to lassitude
and night shivers me to action

My hair burdens yet saves me
from the blistering desert
hoping
I will find the ending

Fringed with possibilities
I will seek the silken cords
slide into the weave of this tale,
held and retold
captured by my tale's tapestry

Ripening

My belly swelling, a resplendent fruit
I cannot escape
the shadowed flutters, my fear
isolation gnaws me
opens the leeched blue void
above my head

I burrow when the sun refuses
to leave me be
I pull dried leaves
old bones
a scrap of bark to be my canopy

How can a person be immersed
in a terrifying sea
the incessant tug and pull
from those who will escape my womb

The unrelenting sucking hole
from they who filled my world
why did Aunty sever my golden cord
I never knew her hidden rules
thankful I am for a wind-carved cave

Why did the prince never come for me
the prince—his name—*what is his name*
why can't I find his name
the sun beats down
pounds me mercilessly

Why have they abandoned me
my aunty, the prince
the teaming lands of me

I would include my parents
but they gave me up easily
without a fight
for just a small bite of some green
how I wish I could chew some green
to be so ripe I could consume
the thought of me

Swirling, my brain heated
too much to try and be
always me and only me

I ripen
burst this madness
set free
my loneliness will end
the voices in me
the babies
who will be part of me

Labor

It happens in an instant
    and forever
my world bursts
    knife bright searing
water flooding between my legs
I try to cup the hot fluids
every
    drop precious, saved
      in dried lizard skins

then I'm suspended
blood mixes with sand
time held in each grain
    an image of my past

I need to be present
no one else can help
deserted in this wasteland
I scream to rip   apart
the blistering sky
as I am   torn   asunder

I shriek ... abandonment, loneliness
loss—gushing
my first-born plunks

    upon the woven mat
       made from my hair
    this crowning treasure

taking flinted stone, I slice
the cord
pull this pallid squalling thing
to my breast as tremors seize me

in a corona of heat
I deliver   his hesitant sister
dark as her brother is light
as if she hides
    in his shadow
from this unforgiving land

I wrap them from the scorching sun
my needed sweat   e v a p o r a t I n g
    all strength to   cry

not yet done
I lick blood-crusted fingers
    birth the great liverish organ
rich, glistening
    from my self
it too must be preserved
swathed in cactus husks

I persevere
later, gag down afterbirth

Colleen Anderson

    this cannibalizing so that I may live
        so they may live
  these little loves
     the tiny mouths

there is no time to rest
    I feel no lighter

Fruiting Bodies

After—
    the witch's disowning
    tossed from the tower
    my prince missing
I grow new parts

Instead of independence
I sprout dependents
    claimed by the desert
    my body fruited
    babes become my world

My lovely, pink-eyed boy
    so pale in the bleaching heat
    his sister dark and staring
    as quiet as her brother
    is raucous

By day, I nurture Sol and Luna
    they furiously suck
    my withered teats
    as desiccated by the sun
    and sand as love's absence

At night, hunger bites them
    their cries break the stars
    I harvest carefully
    milk of cactus, lizard, breast
    and oh, how they fight to live

In day's scorching breath
    my once crowning glory
    a woven hair shade canopies us
    they continue, tears evaporating
    as does my hope

These fruiting bodies
    cleave to me
    heat dries my thoughts
    and I dream of lush spores
    lightly floating   away

Sweet fields, lazy sheep
    birds chiming in spring
    mushrooms plump and firm
    springing up where I step
    my lover waiting with full baskets

I wake to terrified squalling
    as they still cling
    to me and I to them
    in the unending vista
    of all-consuming dunes

Endless days and heat
    grit burrows deep
    germinating a fear that soon
    the sun and sand will pluck
    these sweet fruits of my labor

Seeking

It is through the light
that we seek, blinded
by darkness that freezes us
we probe, bruising knuckles on stones
to grasp that which will give us life
vines hunger for sun
roots we reach for
the earth's sweet nutrients

eventually the only true home
I ever knew draws us together

Blinded, he sought by touch
his feet chafing against gritty sand
his hearing straining to sense the shifting
whisper slither of some creature
often sinister
still, he survived
drawn by my lullabies
the soothing song for starving babes

I shed precious water
just to see another living soul
the prince matters little
when I've been courted
by bleak and certain death

At first we aren't much stronger
Together, until my tears fall
upon his eyes, healing him

Then we protect the babes
hunting and sleep and track
our way out of the badlands
we pull granules of sand from our hair
chew the skin off flayed snakes
left to dry

bounty reveals itself
in the meaty leaves of cactus
candy we devour
my share a king's
to give to the babes

We barely touch in the parching light
but find a rhythm that moves us
until the kingdom of thriving green
beckons and envelops us
welcomes us home with soothing
drops of dew

Seasons

We settle, leaves falling
into something—comfort?
the prince and I, who never found
the rhythm of the seasons
let alone each other

The tower was our spring
an exploration blooming
the seeding accidental
as is the way of trees

Though I summered through two births
seasoned under sun and sand
alone, we endure winter
desolation, a landscape scoured

What grasps us now, alive
reunited in the cooling clasp
of impersonal people, a palace
that seizes, freezing me with decisions
decorum I cannot fathom

The seasons are disordered
do not follow the reason
of a world without strife

and I seek summer's searing solace
as fall's constant abandonment
swirls me, intemperate contemplations

We settle in like wood ticks
and venison salted on the shelf
we lie fallow like fields plowed, untouched
waiting, hoping, seeking, unsure of what may grow

We gaze across the hearthfire
shy smiles more hesitant than those heady
days of spring, he climbing my plait
as I welcomed him with hungry arms
a nest of our young limbs entwined

Now when I can be touched
I feel the court's thrum
and hum, a hive of thought and plans
and freedom to roam the halls
I find there are many rows of plowed silence
stones like hedgerows I cannot see over
yet wander alone

Until I find his chamber where we clutch
desperate aloneness, loving awkwardly
hollowly, never sure what words will fill the gap

By day I find it hard to cultivate
the fields of courtiers
twine through the vines of lives that tangle

By night I seek my babes
now cared for by nursemaids
experts not such as me

I stealthily creep to their cribs
sing songs of planting and of harvest
that I once heard in the far fields
though I never dug into thick loam
nor grasped the scratchy stalks of wheat

Now when I seek him, for brief moments
we meet in sunburst of heat, volcanic splendor
to lay awake and cool together, lost in our own realms
each time we try to plant something
that we can nurture, grow together
yet the next day we have moved into a different season

Sargasso

I never knew names mattered
there being only two of us
no need to differentiate
when one is me—and she

I was a cactus in a desert
she a falcon landing time to time
until she plucked and dropped me

Now I'm adrift in an ocean
trying to filter one drop from another

The voices waft and spin
the air filled
like gnats upon the water

This expanse of names circles me
on an island of unknowing
shall I throw myself in
float upon this sea of words
seek a cool balm

I fear though
that each one is barbed

hooks to flay my flesh
small sharp teeth that latch on

Will unseen, reaching tendrils
names growing out of proportion
tangle me and pull me down
feast on me until
I am sculpted anew

I've only called him Prince
as if that were his name
that was all I needed
in the tower
in the desert

I only named the babes
more a fantasy
than a need

But in this teeming sargasso
I cannot absorb the names
they fill my mouth
drown me
and I must swim
for freedom

Garden

On good days
people everywhere
like wild dandelions
a thousand sunflower faces

But on bad days
more frequently of late
they are mushrooms dispersing spores
saturating the air with words
    muffling, cloying
    my head throbbing
    there is no room for me
    in this miasma

    I cannot

I am the lone tree
in a rampant meadow
of raging splendor
    my eyes skitter over colors
    textures, constant movement
    burrs that hitch to my side

Vomit
crawl into the wardrobe

dark oak walls hold me
safe, quiet, dormant
away from the constant crowd

Wasn't this what I craved
to establish roots
to be one flower in a garden of many
so vibrant it took my breath

Not feel infested
rootbound
fed upon
more adrift than ever

    I flee

Wreath

My hands work clearly, blindly
binding hair, twigs, flowers
tears that cannot nourish nor undo

Is there one moment on life's winding vine
where the stem notches and bends
where blight and incursion gouge and score
turn us down a different path?

Is there one moment
so luminous it obliterates all others
an event so overwhelming
it stunts forward momentum
sets an endless loop for all time?

My life entwined with others
after a long endless cycle
of isolation, the scars and knots
marked the trail of my survival
my fingers twist and twine these tales

>My little boy, Sol, so bright so pale
>bravely holding his light, his namesake
>I clutched him to me, willing strength
>though he brought about my eclipse

I could not keep him in this fecund land
from the kiss of the abyss
my hands gripped nothing
tore at the tangles
of my tenacious unstoppable hair
ever its own snare

I insisted burying him by hand
scooping earth's moist crust
over his swaddled form
so I wouldn't pull out my heart

The ring now curves in, reliving what is fleeting
as I ravel this wreath with my hair and wheat
what little there is of his soft locks
I add asphodel and cowslip for his sweet life
wood for all that abraded
twigs and stones for his flesh and bones

He never asked to live this life
Yet, daily he conquered howling hunger
infused my purpose to nurture
gave unquestioning love
when only desolation prowled, circling us
until we found safety in the realm

We dream and the wreath weaves itself

For Sol, I can crown his victories
his short time visiting
his triumphs against death's voracious mouth

This wreath is for you, little one
wear it well to your next life
cross through the door of shades
ready to meet and conquer
what you couldn't
on this side

Bleeding Hearts

Some plants thrive
in loamy mossy bosoms
while others live bristly defiance
in desert dunes
even the most precious bloom
capitulates to time
lush petals paling falling
floral scent sucked away
fluids drained to feed the earth

My babe fought so hard to be
those first frightful days
struggling through a year
in the castle's cloistered walls
but Sol's slender frame succumbed,
his light fading too quickly

Grief eclipsed me
I cherished Luna all the more
yet the mortared stone imprisoned
my breath caught, suspended
from change

I drooped, visiting often
the tiny hump of dirt

that marked Sol's dormancy
a part of me had died
split in two

Luna thrived, defiant
and I wondered
if I had mixed their names
she bloomed dark and vibrant
while he had been bleached
would the moon's touch have been gentler

I could not reconcile these two halves
the prince's love and mine
a child dead and one alive
a court, a busy hive
my solitary silence of the tower's vigil

The prince's kingdom buzzed
while mine contained plants and birds
and half of my offspring

Luna spun around the prince
I moved into hibernation
the meadow of so many unknown lives
crowding my heart, my breath squeezed
into a tiny seed

I left it and bid goodbye
husband and daughter
remained to grow
and I to recede

In the End

I do not belong to the witch
I do not belong to my prince
I do not belong to this kingdom

I have no people
I have only the tower

It owns me
My protector
My prison

I was never free

Adrift

I was a seed, nurtured
pruned in a garden of seclusion

the witch, a raptor landing
who plucked and dropped me

a cactus in a desert, blooming
carried back in the prince's hands

to an orchard of confusion
now I'm a leaf adrift on the wind

will I stay afloat or drown
spiraling beyond reach

Colleen Anderson

Full Circle

I am back where I began
was it all for nothing
I am emptied, a circle round
unfilled sphere

I began alone but for the witch
now, my aunt, my prince
my children are all gone
though it was I who removed myself

Am I the emptiness
about which the ring revolves
ever turning
into the hollow

Will I find a new cycle
or settle into nothingness
the hole that keeps me here
that no one ever fills

Circles are good
seen as life renewing
but they are the same thing
always repeating

my season is the same
longing, dreams
spinning away

The wheel turns
as I stand still

Loom

This loom of oak and walnut
like a rack for torture
will coerce me to tell my tale

The warp is set, the foundation
where my life took different turns
the immovable moments in time

Some threads are of the finest silk
worm-spun and gifted me
others teased off sheep by birds
or seeds broken down by mice
to bring me flaxen strands

I have combed and spun each one
added my coarse gold
yarns comparing these long years
the span of my life

Upon this frame I weave the tales
nature's gift, the stories
as my tears become the mordant
setting each color
rainbowing walls and loom
brightness dyeing my exile

I shuttle the weft threads
standing over the loom
see the swath of those who came before
the world in my cloistered room

With beater, I mercilessly push the weft
to where it must always be
tight against the warp, held
by this immutable loom
upon which I've been stretched and pulled

For all my isolation, deserted
in a barren land and tower-held
there is one yarn more evident
that I grasp when the sun wanes
and night's bleakness stains the strands

I have lived
I have held fears and hopes
I have loved
when I finish
the loom and tapestry
my story will remain

Reflection

When I left, foregoing
privilege, prestige
a life of ease
he gave me a great silvered mirror

To see those you miss
just speak the names
those people will appear

In early morn
I stare at the shimmering glass
my hands chafed
by warp and weft of loom

Fevered, I press my hands upon the cool glass
dreaming that I can break this membrane
push through to any time

    Our daughter grows strong
    a raven willful, knowing no boundaries
    those will come in time
    a kingdom's destiny twined

Some days I try to fathom the distance
I can wish anywhere I know

to anyone I've seen
but there are few places, a desert, a tower, a palace
and cherished people number one hand

When solitude spills
a quiet flood to wash away my sanity
at the edge of delirium
I lay upon the floor, hang on

When stars jewel the dark sky
the vast expanse noticing me
I let them rain, saturate
fill my void

Knowing it brings starlight
potential, something that scares me
into accepting the stone's embrace
my living crypt
my choosing

Seeds

the daisy falls apart
petals pulling loose
wilting in a heartbeat
an intake
an inhalation
a moment
forever

I clutch the seeds
I hold and hold and hold
feeling the years
drift away
chances for something new

loneliness shadows me
a cooling that makes it hard
to furrow my future
possibilities for planting
new paths

the change I seek
robbed by a wind's breath of fear
seeds aloft above my head
floating free
unlike me

these stones box me
seeds drop from my hand
drying up
unable to be
the change I need
to grow

Spring

I have settled into the weave
slowly wearing the fabric of my life
color, texture slowly massaged by sunlight
and time, eventually consumed
into powder and dust
I accept this, my time
alone but for my human sentinels
who keep me fed
shelter from the leering sky

Yet my heart hammers hollow
tattoos that echo
of a life I brushed against
never truly touched

Until a tantalizing breeze wends
softly through my bower
the mirror's surface shimmers
while my servants and I clean
dust gently, dislodging graying cobwebs
a puff of my dried-out past

We throw open windows
allow in birdsong
breaths of spring blossoms

high in the tower's dovecote
I look out upon the land
awaiting something
I know not what

My life is about to change
shift directions
bloom in ways I cannot know

Tide

the world trembles the door
breath frozen in my chest's cage
as a servant cracks the way—
a knight swathed in midnight skies

a star's distant glimmer burns
in my heart, his eyes smolder
this man holding shadows
spilling curls upon his brow

clouds eclipse moon and senses
dredging beneath the tidal surge
feelings long left beached, unfurl
my clammed tongue breaches

air redolent, awaiting, unsure
I beckon him to spend the night
anchor here before he embarks
Launcelot sailing tournament's way

one look harpoons my need
pries open damaged, hidden dreams
his good nature polishes sea glass
reveals pearls of my life submerged

I've known men who command the sun
my prince, a beacon on lonely shores
yet this man nets unknown needs
hesitation tangles my wish to dive

I will surge above the waves of fear
ride the urge to plunge these depths
in turn he gives me pirate's gold
with turns of phrase and faience gems

he looks into my eyes, this storm
absorbs my siren song, the cast offs
that we wish to hold, be bold enough
to discover broken flights across the seas

his tales anchor me, shields against
the howling sky, emboldens me to dare
can I plumb the vistas of my wants
never touched, nor quite free

I cannot be the grain embedded
in this stone shell that's become my life
I must crack asunder expectations
swim strong against the societal tide

when Launcelot leaves for tournament
he wears my favor on his sleeve
a clarion call that I'm in this world
a woman now who can sail the storms

I stand beneath the tower's weight staring
into the unfurling sky, knowing now
though he is gone, he will return
our fates now inextricably tied

Tapestry

One maid, a carter, a cook
my companions to supply
spindles, linen, wool and food
bring them to my tower rooms
where I feverishly work

The great loom fills one turret
my masterwork progresses

My tongue is twined with dust and sorrow
rarely can I breach small talk
but I try, to keep my voice
from fraying

I dye the strands, hum
look upon my mirror, reflect
my days, a tapestry I weave
with the golden yarn
of my ever-growing hair
my one true treasure, my burden

Like cloth of gold, the strands add glimmer
each woven image shifts ever so subtly
the people captured in my life's banner
eyes following the maid across the room

she asks me to cover them when sweeping,
edging ever farther from mirror and loom

My warp is weighted within this tower
the stones that surround
have always anchored me

All other threads, incomplete
' til they reveal my story
      childhood dreams of escape
      my prince and children
      the desperate desiccation of the desert
      the crowded halls of a bustling kingdom
      the dark stabbing heat of Launcelot

I create many small tapestries
scenes of a limited life
of a world I enriched with fantasy

Someday I will finish the weave
my tale's tapestry
the fringe added, always leaving
possibilities of what might have been

Autumn

They bring him to my tower
not dead, not quite alive
Launcelot hanging on

Like a leaf that curls, color-changing
eventually drifting away
the tree bereft of its jewels
veined with experience

From my bower, I watch them falling
    ever falling, these moments
        a cloying prison
        a desert wasteland
        a bustling castle
        a stately tower
        a lonely recluse
        a noble nurse
        a gallant knight
        a free yet burdened man

Until they land
waiting for winter's clock

Launcelot languishes
I stitch and soothe

work to mend him
sunlight tastes his face
warming my soul

At my loom
I wait and work
tales of what is and could have been
what never was

He wakes, gains health
telling me of the world outside
Camelot, noble pursuits
like the books upon my shelves
yet more real and solid

I fall again
not thrust into the world
from the tower
my betrayer my heart
yet fall I do

The day I dread comes
hale, he stands tall, not yet ready
to leave the tree of life

For your kindness, a boon I shall give
He says as he straps on greaves
and breastplate over a heart
already unreachable

This small gem, I asked for only one
To take me as wife
(in secret) if he must
knowing already
I can only be a wife in shadow

Armored to take on the world
he cannot save my life
reveals his own dark vein
the queen who holds his heart
he leaves

I fall

Winter

I must abandon
my past, the tower, the witch
my little loves
the prince and all who twined me
the tangled tale, this hair that braided my fate

Shorn, hooded and cloaked, I hunch
beneath the bleaking sky
guided by silent servants
to the boat upon the river
the pod to carry this lonely pea

I have escaped the stone coop
no longer able to contain me
in my bower, the silvered mirror cracks
reverberates and shudders the trees
heartbreak and release

leaves flutter, fall, former glory dimmed
and nuts plunk upon the ground
silence now, my final shroud
the loom is empty, tapestry complete

I'm past the seasons of my youth alone
when I budded with the prince

cozied comfort of orchid, lilac, savory sage
that grew promises in me

Until the blistering banishment
a summering bleached and bled
becoming mother before I'd flown free
abandoned, desolate, again

The fall of my days when I withered
trying to be wife, a mother
a princess in a thriving realm
and yet never had I taken hold
no rooting in the soils of my life
no comfort among the murmuring
of courtly life, a blight I could only flee

To come upon my wintering
endless days weaving, thinking
staring into the great silvered mirror
to watch life pass me by

Launcelot, that last faint hope
pollinated love that had lain dormant
but even that is not enough

I slip now into the wooden pod
this slim canoe my deliverance
my open sarcophagus
lidded by the howling sky

Robbed of breath, my heart thuds
then cracks in two, as did the mirror
reflecting on my past

I will sail on to Camelot
let Launcelot gaze upon me
one last time
grant me grace

A peace at last, perhaps new growth
free of enchantments
swaddled well from the uncaring sky
he will plant me deep within the earth

Acknowledgements

Thank you to my poetry crit group, Brian Hugenbruch, Elizabeth Shack, Marie Brennan and Kathy Schrenk, who saw many of these poems and offered useful suggestions. They made me a better poet. Thanks also to Stephanie Wytowich, who had faith in this project and for her editing, and Jennifer Barnes for layout, at Raw Dog Screaming Press.

Previously Published

Thank you to the follow publishers who previously published these poems:

"Fruiting Bodies"*Journ-E 3.2*
"Locks"*Abyss and Apex #84*
"Small Reveals"*Amazing Stories*
"Wreath"*Star*Line 47.4*

About the Author

Multiple award-nominated and award-winning author Colleen Anderson has been widely published across seven countries, with works appearing in respected publications such as *Weird Tales, Cemetery Dance, Amazing,* and the award-winning *Shadow Atlas.* Her Rhysling Award-winning poem "Machine (r)Evolution" was featured in Tenebrous Press's *Brave New Weird,* and she is a two-time winner of the SFPA's dwarf poetry contest. Based in Vancouver, BC, she has been a Canada Council, BC Arts Council and Ladies of Horror Fiction grant recipient. Her poetry collections include *The Lore of Inscrutable Dreams, I Dreamed a World,* and *Weird Worlds,* as well as fiction collections *A Body of Work* and *Embers Amongst the Fallen*—all of which are available online. *Vellum Leaves and Lettered Skins* is her fourth collection. She is working on two other poetry collections and fiction collections.

www.ingramcontent.com/pod-product-compliance
Lightning Source LLC
LaVergne TN
LVHW041341080426
835512LV00006B/563